JOHN JACOB NILES
CHRISTMAS SONGS AND CAROLS

12 SELECTIONS, INCLUDING 6 NEW ARRANGEMENTS OF APPALACHIAN CAROLS COLLECTED BY JOHN JACOB NILES

ED 4397
First Printing: June 2008

ISBN 978-1-4234-3695-9

G. SCHIRMER, Inc.

DISTRIBUTED BY
HAL•LEONARD®
CORPORATION
7777 W. BLUEMOUND RD. P.O. BOX 13819 MILWAUKEE, WI 53213

www.schirmer.com
www.halleonard.com

PREFACE

This collection includes Christmas selections drawn from *The Songs of John Jacob Niles*, and new arrangements for voice and piano of six further carols. The source for these new arrangements was the 1935 G. Schirmer publication:

Ten Christmas Carols from the Southern Appalachian Mountains collected and simply arranged with accompaniment for piano by John Jacob Niles

Unlike his fuller settings, such as "I Wonder as I Wander," Niles created a very simple piano accompaniment for one verse only of each of the carols in *Ten Christmas Carols*, with lyrics printed separately for all remaining verses. This is a wonderful source, but is not a particularly good performing edition. Our purpose in this new edition of six of the carols from *Ten Christmas Carols* was to use Niles' work for the basis of fuller settings that would be suitable for performance. Some verses were eliminated in these new arrangements. We made a conscious effort to attempt to stay true to Niles' basic harmonization in these new arrangements.

John Jacob Niles collected these Appalachian carols by recording singers in various locations. Comments about carols with new arrangements in this collection are cited below.

Down in yon forest
Recorded in Cherokee County, North Carolina, date unknown.

The Seven Joys of Mary
Recorded in Cherokee County, North Carolina, 1933.

Lulle Lullay
Recorded at "Old-Timers Day" in Gatlinburg, Tennessee, June 16, 1934. Niles commented that it was recorded "from the singing of an old lady known to me only as 'the old lady with the gray hat.' It is my belief that this song from the Shapenote singers."

See Jesus the Saviour
Recorded in Index, Morgan County, Kentucky, May, 1913.

Jesus the Christ is born
Recorded near Pitman Center, Sevier County, Tennessee, June, 1934.

The Cherry-Tree
Recorded in Breathitt County, Kentucky, May, 1934.

For contemporary comprehension, occasional words were changed in the songs above for this edition. A very few words have been changed in the remaining songs to adapt them for general use.

John Jacob Niles's comments about other songs included this collection:

The Carol of the Birds
"I wrote 'Carol of the Birds' for my older son, Tom, when he was four years old."

The Flower of Jesse
"...is based on a poem written by a man I respect enormously, long dead...James Ryman blind and deaf, the chaplain at Hopemount Abbey in England... This is my adaptation of James Ryman's poem written at the turn of the fifteenth century. I wrote the text and the tune... You may discover that I write the accompaniment as if I were writing for a string quartet. I like to hear all four voices going and not just standing still, moving and getting somewhere, adding something vital to the support of the melodic line.

I wonder as I wander
"'I wonder as I wander' grew out of three lines of music sung for me by a girl who called herself Annie Morgan. The place was Murphy, North Carolina, and the time was July, 1933. The Morgan family, revivalists all, were about to be ejected by the police, after having camped in the town square for some little time, cooking, washing, hanging their wash from the Confederate monument and generally conducting themselves in such a way as to be classed a public nuisance. Preacher Morgan and his wife pled poverty; they had to hold one more meeting in order to buy enough gas to get out of town. It was then that Annie Morgan came out a tousled, unwashed blond, and very lovely. She sang the first three lines of the verse of 'I wonder as I wander.' At twenty-five cents a performance, I tried to get her to sing all the song. After eight tries, all of which are carefully recorded in my notes, I had only three lines of verse, a garbled fragment of melodic material and a magnificent idea. With the writing of additional verses and the development of the original melodic material, 'I wonder as I wander' came into being. I sang it for five years in my concerts before it caught on. Since then, it has been sung by soloists and choral groups wherever the English language is spoken and sung."

Jesus, Jesus, rest your head
"...came into being because my mother and I visited a family named the Grahams, who, at the turn of the century, lied in Hardin County, Kentucky. my mother noted down a 'little Christmas song' they sang, for I was too young at the time to take it down myself. About 1909, after I had written 'Go 'way from My Window,' my mother game me a few slips of jumbled notes and said, 'Here, see if you can make a song out of this.' 'Jesus, Jesus, rest your head' was the result."

What Songs Were Sung
"...written for the late Gladys Swarthout and first performed by her."

Richard Walters
editor
June, 2008

CONTENTS

		Performance Track	Accompaniment Track

APPALACHIAN CAROLS
Collected by John Jacob Niles

SONGS
Composed by John Jacob Niles

Performers on the CD: [1] **Kathleen Sonnentag, mezzo-soprano**
[2] **Kurt Ollmann, baritone**
Richard Walters, piano

THE CHERRY-TREE

Adapted and arranged for voice and piano by
Bryan Stanley

Collected and arranged by
John Jacob Niles

meek - ness, Then Mar - y what was _ mild, so mild, Said: "Cher - ries are the _

best _ thing, For wom - en bear - in' child." 4. Then

up spake Jo - seph to Mar - y— He _ was a man un - kind, un - kind—"Oh,
(5.) tell this one, and _ straight - way, That cher - ries ain't noth - in' to me, to me; If

1.

it's who has sired your _ ba - by, That's a - both - er - in' my mind. 5. Go
he's e'er a man to _ sire a child, He's a man to climb a

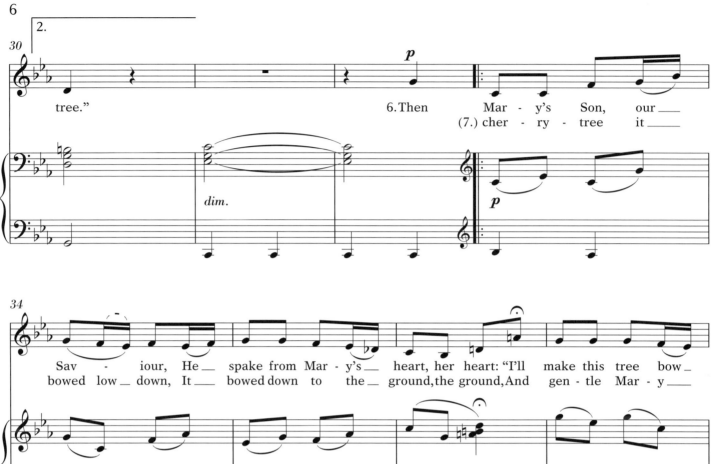

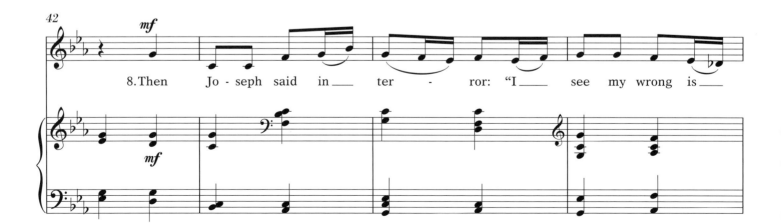

30

2.

tree." 6. Then Mar - y's Son, our ___
(7.) cher - ry - tree it ___

34

Sav - iour, He ___ spake from Mar - y's ___ heart, her heart: "I'll make this tree bow ___
bowed low ___ down, It ___ bowed down to the ___ ground, the ground, And gen - tle Mar - y ___

38

1.　**2.**

low ___ down, I'll take my ma - ma's part." 7. Then the
helped her - self To cher - ries with - out a sound.

42

mf

8. Then Jo - seph said in ___ ter - ror: "I ___ see my wrong is ___

great, is great, Pray come my gen - tle ___ Queen of Heav'n, The se - cret do re -

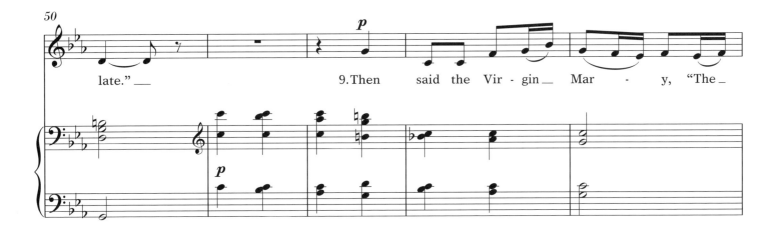

late." ___　　　　　　9. Then said the Vir - gin ___ Mar - y, "The ___

se - cret I will ___ share, will share: On Christ-mas Eve in an ox - 's stall, The Christ-Child I will

bear,　　On Christ-mas Eve, in an ox - 's stall, The Christ-Child I will bear."

LULLE LULLAY

Adapted and arranged for voice and piano by
Bryan Stanley

Collected and arranged by
John Jacob Niles

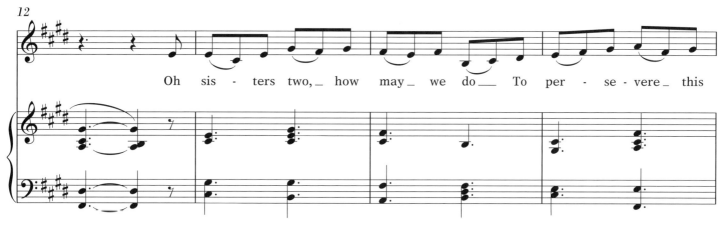

Oh sis - ters two,_ how may_ we do_ To per - se - vere_ this

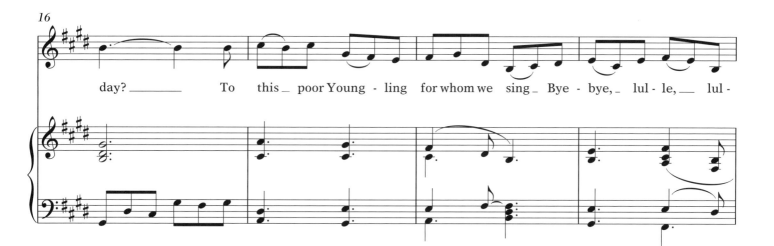

day?_____ To this_ poor Young - ling for whom we sing_ Bye - bye,_ lul - le,_ lul -

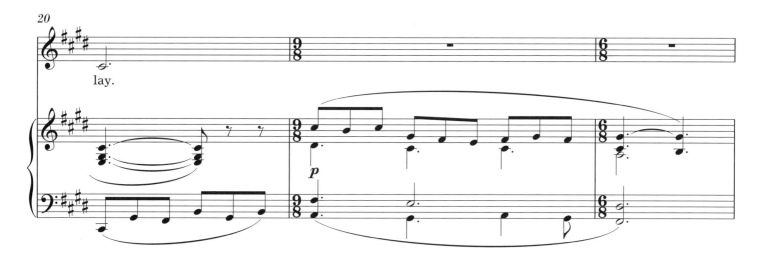

lay.

Her - od the King,____ in __ his rag - ing, Charged __ he hath this day ____ His

sol - diers in __ their strength __ and might __ All chil - dren young __ to slay. _____ Then

woe __ is me __ poor child __ for Thee, _ And ev - er mourn __ and

say, _____ For at ___ thy part - ing nor say nor sing __ Bye -

bye, _ lul - le, ___ lul - lay.

And when the stars in-gath - er do, In their far ven - ture stay, Then smile as dream - ing, Lit - tle One, Bye - bye, lul - le, lul - lay, bye - bye, lul - le, lul - lay.

DOWN IN YON FOREST

Adapted and arranged for voice and piano by
Bryan Stanley

Collected and arranged by
John Jacob Niles

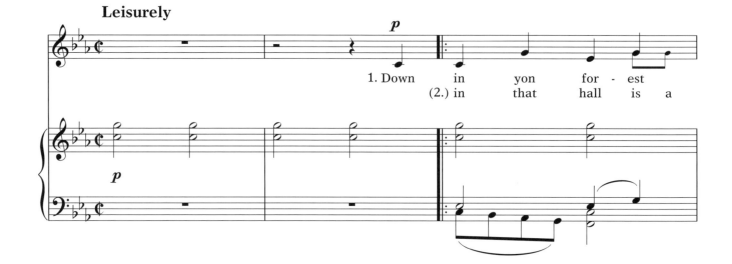

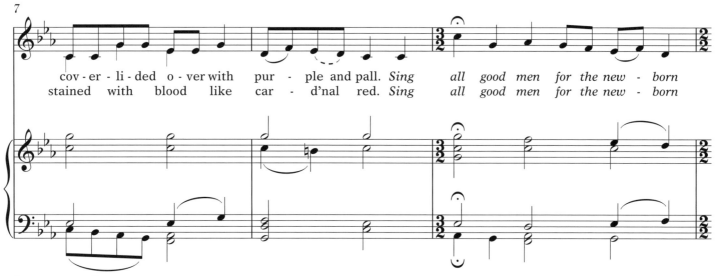

*a mattress of straw

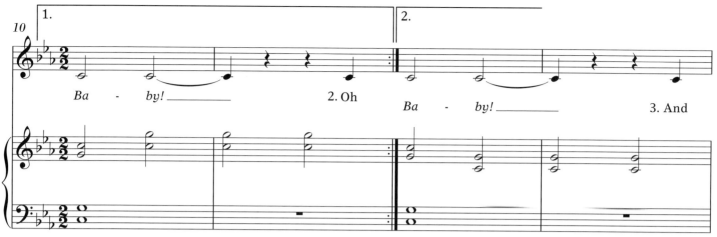

Ba - by! _____ 2. Oh Ba - by! _____ 3. And

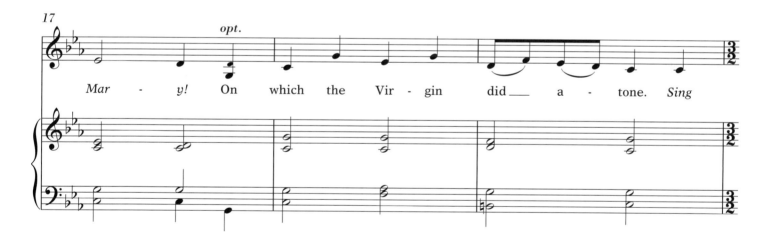

at that pal - let is___ a___ stone, Sing May, Queen May, sing

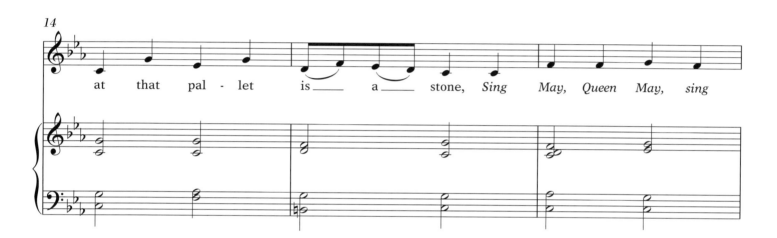

Mar - y! On which the Vir - gin did___ a - tone. Sing

all good men for the new - born Ba - by! _____ 4. Un -

der that hall is a gush - ing flood: *Sing May, Queen May, sing*

Mar - y! From Christ's own side 'tis wa - ter and blood. Sing

all good men for the new - born Ba - by!

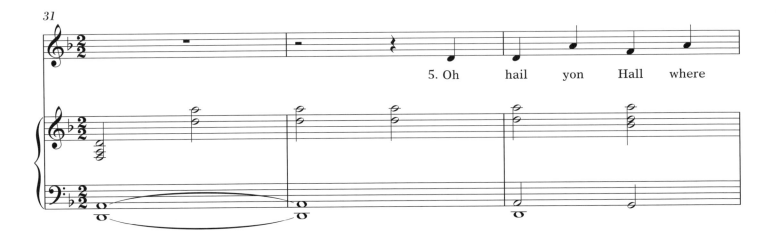

5. Oh hail yon Hall where

JESUS THE CHRIST IS BORN

Adapted and arranged for voice and piano by
Bryan Stanley

Collected and arranged by
John Jacob Niles

Majestic, though spirited

Je - sus the Christ is born, Give thanks now, ev' - ry one. Re -
joice, ye great ones and ye _ small, God's will, it has been done. ___ Ye might - y kings of
earth, Be - fore the man - ger bed, Cast down, cast down your gold - en _ crown From

off your roy - al head.

_mp_

For in this low - ly

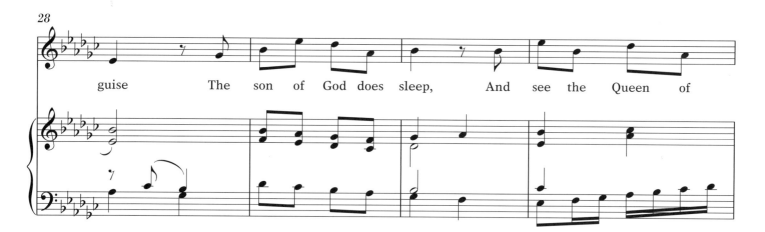

guise The son of God does sleep, And see the Queen of

Heav - en kneel, Her faith-ful vig - il keep._____ Two an-gels at His

head, Two an-gels at His feet, Be-side His bed the flow-er__ red, Per-

fum-ing there so sweet.

Je-sus the Christ is born, Give thanks now, ev'-ry one. Re-

joice, ye great ones and ye__ small, God's will, it has been done.__

THE SEVEN JOYS OF MARY

Adapted and arranged for voice and piano by
Richard Walters

Collected and arranged by
John Jacob Niles

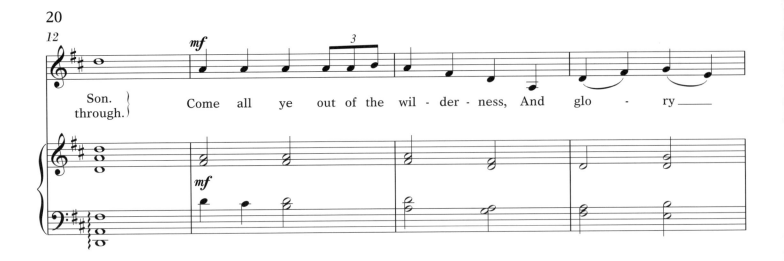

Son. / through. Come all ye out of the wil - der - ness, And glo - ry

be, Fa - ther, Son, and the Ho - ly Ghost, Through all e - ter - ni -

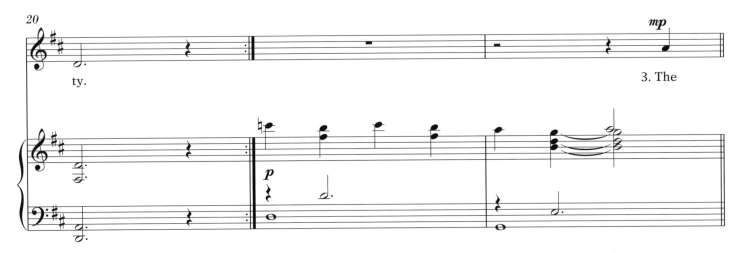

ty. 3. The

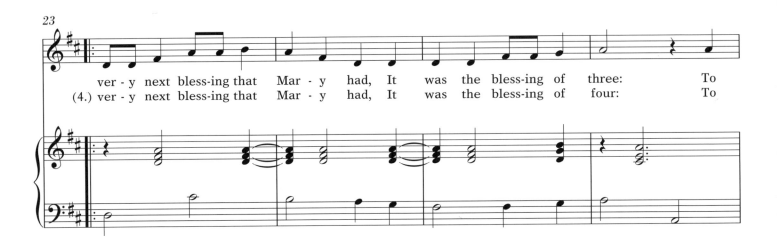

ver - y next bless-ing that Mar - y had, It was the bless-ing of three: To
(4.) ver - y next bless-ing that Mar - y had, It was the bless-ing of four: To

27
think her lit - tle Je - sus Could make the blind to see, Could
think her lit - tle Je - sus Could make the rich to poor, Could

31
1.
make the blind to see. 4. The
2.
make the rich to poor.

35
mp
5. The ver - y next bless - ing that Mar - y had, It
(6.) ver - y next bless - ing that Mar - y had, It
mp

38
was the bless - ing of five: To think her lit - tle
was the bless - ing of six: To think her lit - tle

Je - sus Could make the dead to rise, Could
Je - sus Could make the well to sick, Could

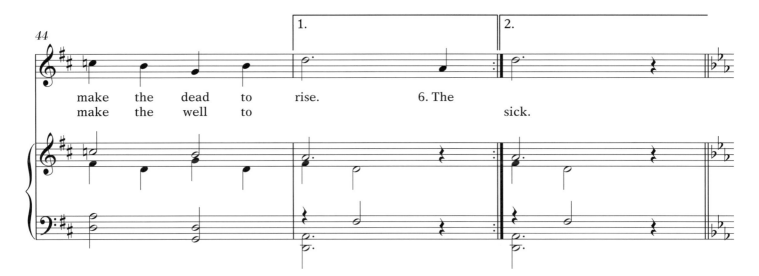

make the dead to rise. 6. The
make the well to sick.

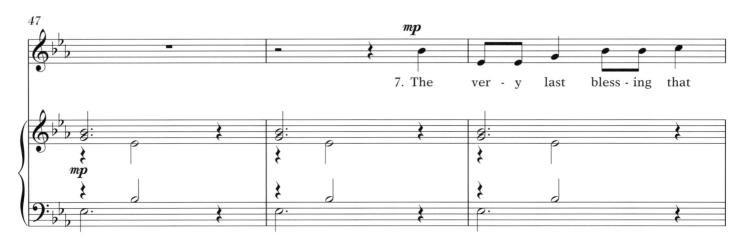

7. The ver - y last bless - ing that

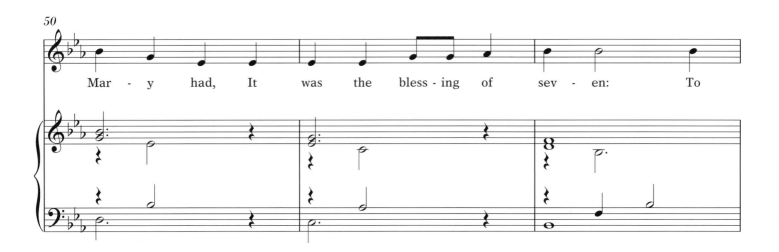

Mar - y had, It was the bless - ing of sev - en: To

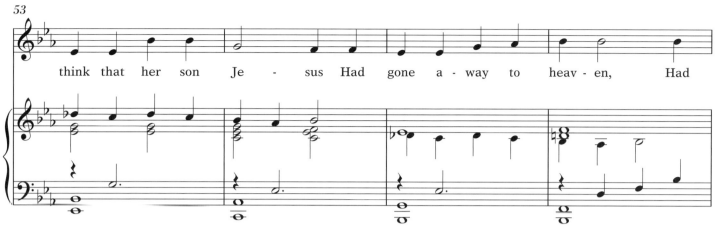

think that her son Je - sus Had gone a - way to heav - en, Had

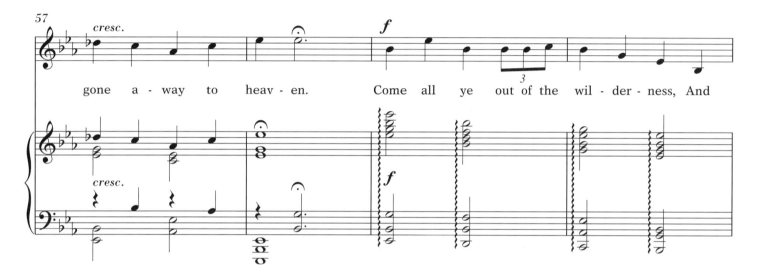

cresc.   ⌢   *f*

gone a - way to heav - en. Come all ye out of the wil - der - ness, And

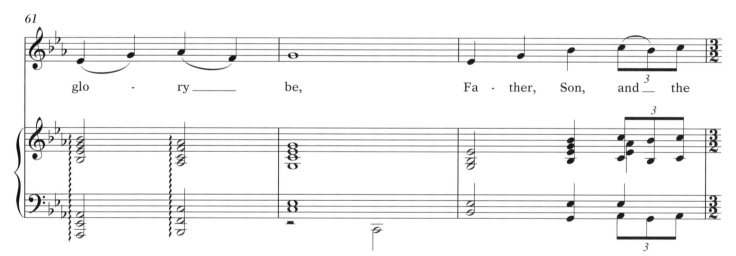

glo - ry _____ be,   Fa - ther, Son, and _ the

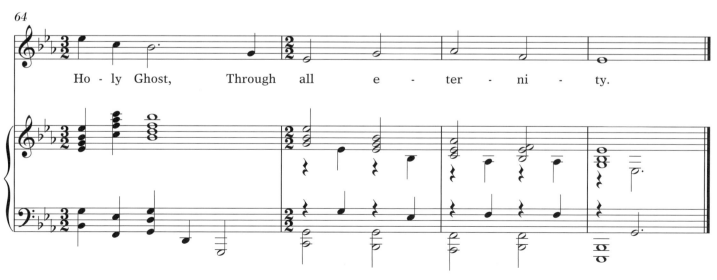

Ho - ly Ghost, Through all e - ter - ni - ty.

SEE JESUS THE SAVIOUR

Adapted and arranged for voice and piano by
Bryan Stanley

Collected and arranged by
John Jacob Niles

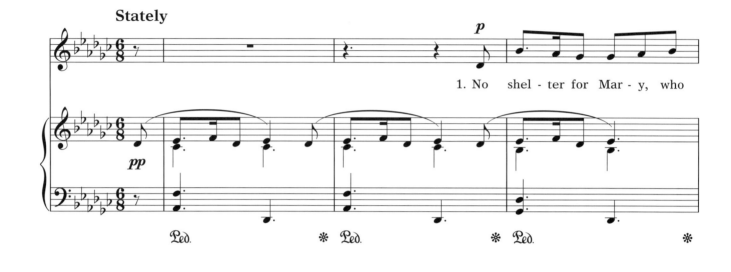

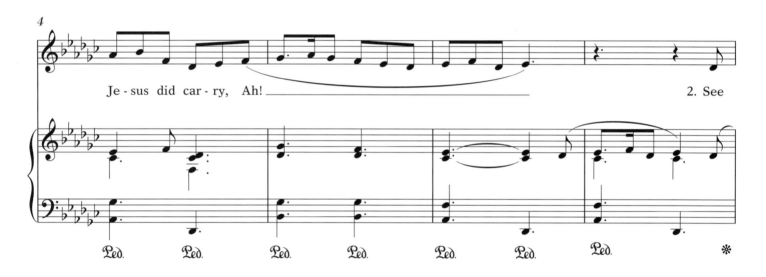

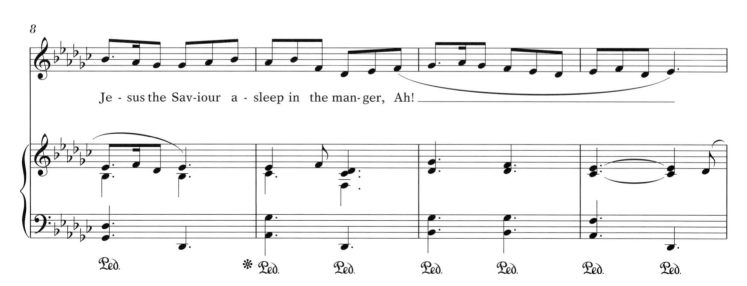

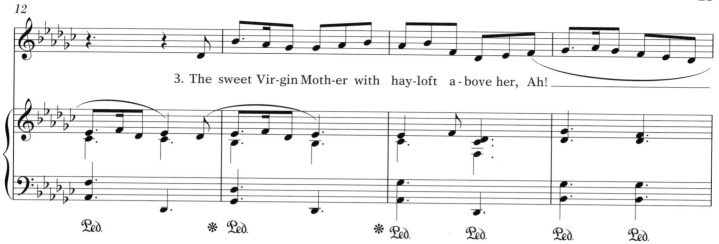

3. The sweet Vir-gin Moth-er with hay-loft a-bove her, Ah! _____

Ped.   ✻ Ped.   ✻ Ped.   Ped.   Ped.   Ped.

4. The wise men at mid-night did

Ped.   sim.

fol-low the stars' light, Ah! _____   5. The

shep-herds came pray-ing, the Scrip-tures o-bey-ing, Ah! _____

for Gladys Swarthout

THE CAROL OF THE BIRDS

Words and Music by
John Jacob Niles

In graceful, pastoral style

mf

Oh a man - y a bird___ did wake and fly, cu -

roo, cu - roo, ___ cu - roo, ___ Oh a man - y a bird___ did

wake and fly To the man - ger bed with a wan - der - ing cry On

Christ - mas day in the morn - ing, cu - roo, cu - roo, cu -

roo, _____ cu - roo, cu - roo, ___ cu - roo. _____ The _

lark, the dove, __ the red - bird came, cu - roo, cu - roo, ___ cu -

roo, _____ The _ lark, the dove, __ the red - bird came And

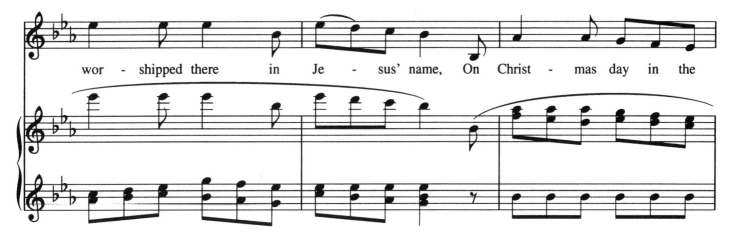

wor - shipped there in Je - sus' name, On Christ - mas day in the

morn - ing, cu - roo, cu - roo, cu - roo,_____ cu -

roo, cu - roo,__ cu - roo._____ The_ owl was there,_ his

eyes so wide, cu - roo, cu - roo,_____ cu - roo,_____ The_

owl was there, __ his eyes so wide As he did sit at

sweet Ma - ry's side On Christ - mas day in the morn - ing, cu -

roo, cu - roo, cu - roo, __ cu - roo, cu - roo, __ cu -

roo. __ The __ shep - herd knelt __ up - on the hay, cu -

roo, cu - roo, _____ cu - roo, _____ The _ shep - herd knelt _ up -

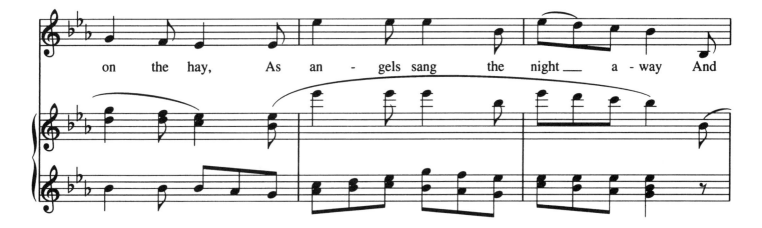

on the hay, As an - gels sang the night _ a - way And

God pro - claim - ed the ho - ly day, cu - roo, cu - roo, cu -

roo, _____ cu - roo, cu - roo, _ cu - roo. _____

THE FLOWER OF JESSE

Words and Music by
John Jacob Niles

Flowing and with great tenderness ♩ = 72

There _ is a flow'r sprung of a tree, the root there-of is

called Jes - se. 'Tis in - deed a flow'r of Pre-cious Price for _

there is none _ such in all of _ Par - a - dise. _

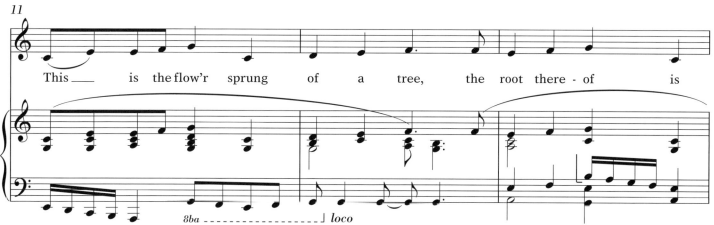

This ___ is the flow'r sprung of a tree, the root there - of is

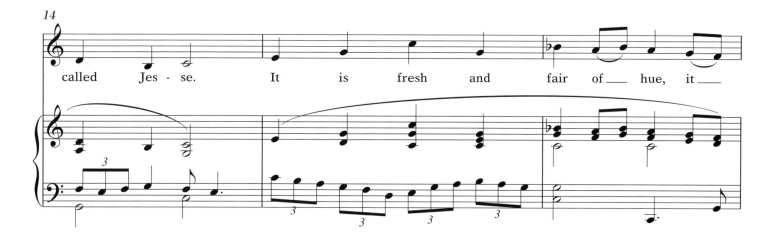

called Jes - se. It is fresh and fair of ___ hue, it ___

nev - er ___ fad - eth but is ___ ev - er new. ___ This ___ is a flow - er sprung

rit.   a tempo

of a tree, the root there - of is called Jes - se.

There is a flow'r sprung

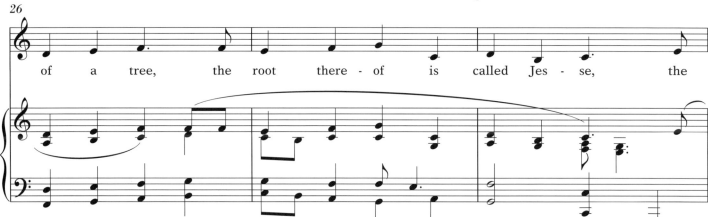

of a tree, the root there - of is called Jes - se, the

seed there - of, the seed was God's com - mand

sown it was by his own hand.

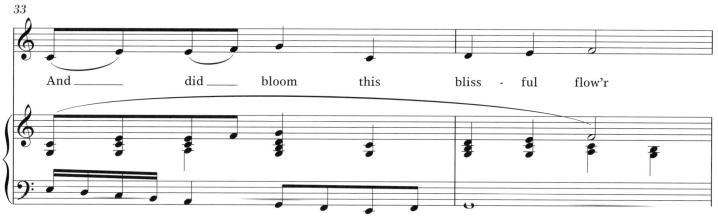

And _____ did _____ bloom this bliss - ful flow'r

Just be - side sweet Mar - y's bow'r.*

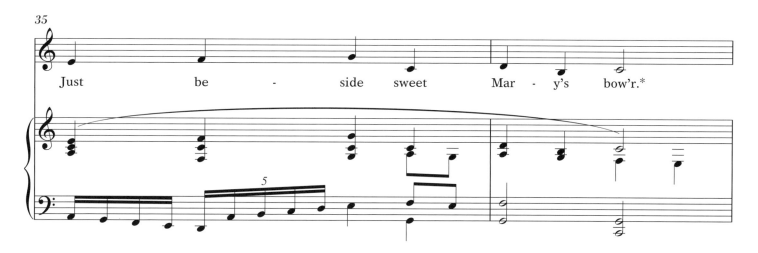

Come ev - 'ry one in _____ our _____ coun - try, Hon - or the flow'r of good Jes -

se, _____ good Jes - se. _____

rit.

*a rustic dwelling

for Thomas Michael Tolliver Niles on being five years of age

JESUS, JESUS, REST YOUR HEAD

Adapted from the singing
of three people in Hardin County, Kentucky

Adapted by
John Jacob Niles

All the mor - tal folk on earth Sleep in feath - ers at their birth.

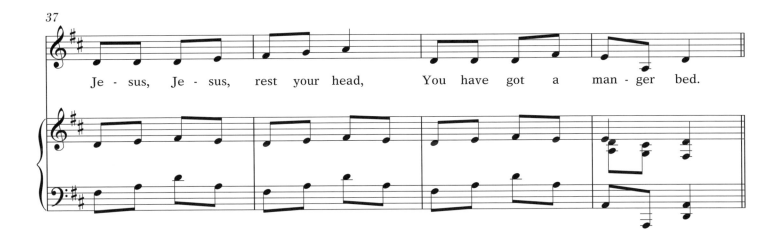

Je - sus, Je - sus, rest your head, You have got a man - ger bed.

2. To that man - ger came then wise men, Bring - ing things from hin and yon.

For the moth - er and the fa - ther And the bless - ed lit - tle Son.

Milk-maids left their fields and flocks And sat be-side the ass and ox.

Je - sus, Je - sus, rest your head, You have got a man - ger bed.

All the mor - tal folk on earth Sleep in feath - ers at their birth.

Je - sus, Je - sus, rest your head, You have got a man - ger bed.

SWEET LITTLE BOY JESUS

Words and Music by
John Jacob Niles

lit - tle boy Je - sus in man-ger so low,____ Sweet lit - tle boy Je - sus, we
place for the Moth - er, no place for the Son,____ No place for to rest____ the

nev - er did know You were a God and a friend of ours too,____ Sweet
new-ly-birthed one; See how the shep - herds did seek out a shed____ And

lit - tle boy Je - sus   we nev - er knew. _____ 2. No
make in the man - ger the Christ - child a bed. _____ 3. The

ox and the sheep ___ stand si - lent - ly by, ___ While an - gels car - ol - in' did
lit - tle boy Je - sus 'in man - ger so low, ___ Sweet lit - tle boy Je - sus, we

fill up the sky. ___ The folk in the vil - lage slept si - lent - ly on, ___ Not
nev - er did know You were a God and a friend of ours, too, ___ Sweet

Fine

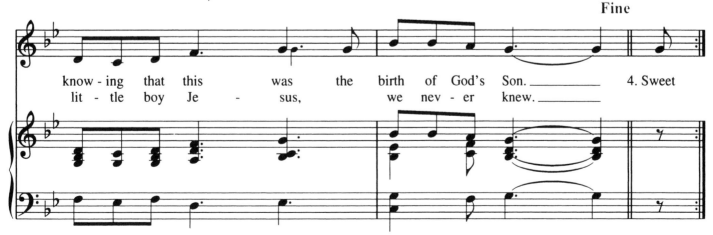

know - ing that this was the birth of God's Son. _____ 4. Sweet
lit - tle boy Je - sus, we nev - er knew. _____

I WONDER AS I WANDER
(Appalachian Carol)

Collected, adapted, and arranged by
John Jacob Niles

Je-sus the Sav-ior did come for to die For poor on-'ry peo-ple like

you and like I... I won-der as I wan-der, out un-der the sky.

When Ma - ry birthed Je - sus, 'twas in a cow's stall, With

wise men and farm - ers and shep - herds and all. But high from God's heav - en a

star's light did fall, And the prom - ise of a - ges it then did re - call.

If Je - sus had want - ed for an - y wee thing, A

star in the sky, or a bird on the wing, Or all of God's an - gels in

heav'n for to sing, He sure - ly could have it, 'cause he was the King.

I won - der as I wan - der, out un - der the sky, How

Je - sus the Sav - ior did come for to die For poor on - 'ry peo - ple like

you and like I... I won - der as I wan - der, out un - der the sky.

WHAT SONGS WERE SUNG

Words and Music by
John Jacob Niles

Tenderly ♩ = c. 66 (in a story-telling manner)

We can-not tell, we do not know What stars shone down so long a-go, When Mar-y birthed her own sweet Son And peace and love be-came as one. The Son of God, as scrip-tures said, Was Vir-gin born in a ti-ny shed, Where sim-ple shep-herds

stood hard by   While heav'n - ly sound   filled   up the sky.   Now

let us stand,   un - cov - ered all,   Be - fore this crèche in _____ low - ly stall,   Where

kings and an - gels dig - ni - fy God's _ gift, His Son, in hu - mil - i - ty.

We do not know,   we can - not tell   What songs were sung,   what _

star-light fell, Or why the ho - ly mys-ter - y stands For so man-y years in

so man - y lands. We can-not tell, we

do not know What stars shone down so ___ long a - go, When Mar - y birthed her

own sweet Son And ___ peace and love be - came as one. ___